STRANGE HISTORY

T0011222

The Peculiar Past in
ANCIENT EGYPT

by Charis Mather

BEARPORT
PUBLISHING

Minneapolis, Minnesota

Credits

Bearport Publishing Company Product Development Team

President: Jen Jenson; Director of Product Development: Spencer Brinker; Managing Editor: Allison Juda; Associate Editor: Naomi Reich; Associate Editor: Tiana Tran; Art Director: Colin O'Dea; Designer: Elena Klinkner; Designer: Kayla Eggert; Product Development Assistant: Owen Hamlin

Library of Congress Cataloging-in-Publication Data is available at www.loc.gov or upon request from the publisher.

ISBN: 979-8-88916-478-4 (hardcover)
ISBN: 979-8-88916-483-8 (paperback)
ISBN: 979-8-88916-487-6 (ebook)

For more information, write to Bearport Publishing, 5357 Penn Avenue South, Minneapolis, MN 55419.

CONTENTS

STRANGE TIME TO BE ALIVE!

What was life like for people in ancient Egypt? Whether they knew it at the time or not, the ancient Egyptians lived in a **peculiar** past!

The civilization in ancient Egypt lasted for thousands of years. Its history stretched so long that during that time, the Great Pyramids were both built and then became ancient history!

Ancient Egypt was amazing in so many ways. But some of the things its people did were absolutely **absurd**.

The deeper you dig into ancient Egypt, the more strange stories you're bound to uncover.

THE POWER PYRAMID

Life in ancient Egypt was very different depending on where you were on the power pyramid of the time. For those low on the pyramid, life could be pretty rough.

Pharaoh

Priests and Nobles

Soldiers

Scribes and Craftspeople

Farmers and Enslaved People

POWERFUL PHARAOHS

Pharaohs were the rulers of ancient Egypt. They were seen as godlike by the people. They spent a lot of their time resolving **religious** matters—sometimes even after they were dead.

Even after he died, people asked a statue of Pharaoh Amenhotep I questions. If the statue moved in a certain way, that meant yes.

Look, he said yes!

Workers

Just below the pharaoh were nobles and priests. These people lived well, but like everyone else, they were still under the pharaoh's rule. Then, there were soldiers, **scribes,** and craftspeople. Farmers, other workers, and **enslaved** people had the least amount of power.

In ancient Egypt, it was nearly impossible to get a better job. However, some people did manage to climb the power pyramid. A man named Horemheb went from being a soldier to becoming pharaoh!

Horemheb

FIT FOR A PHARAOH

Whatever you thought of the power pyramid, it was best to keep any complaints about the pharaoh to yourself. Some pharaohs wore crowns with cobras on them that were said to be able to spit fire at their enemies.

The pharaoh's outfit also included a fake beard. While the weather was often too hot for a real beard, a fake one could be worn when the pharaoh wanted to look impressive.

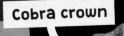

Cobra crown

Most pharaohs were men, but a few women became pharaohs. They sometimes wore fake beards, too!

Queen Hatshepsut's fake beard

With so much power, pharaohs could afford to live very comfortably.

GOLD GALORE

King Tut became pharaoh when he was 9 and ruled until he was 18. He didn't live long, but he died rich. King Tut was buried in a golden coffin inside a room filled with treasure.

STICKY SOLUTIONS

Who wouldn't want gold shoes?

Pharoah Pepi II hated flies. To keep them away, he reportedly covered some of his enslaved people with honey. Pepi II hoped the bothersome bugs would be attracted to the honey instead of him.

PHARAOH FOCUS: CLEOPATRA

Cleopatra was a pharaoh who knew how to get what she wanted. Unfortunately for some, she was not the most peaceful of pharaohs.

Cleopatra

SIBLING STRUGGLES

Cleopatra's brother, Ptolemy XIII, once tried to push her out of power. To get back at him, Cleopatra teamed up with another important ruler, Julius Caesar. The story goes that she went to talk to Caesar in an unusual way. Cleopatra snuck into his room by hiding in a rolled-up carpet.

Talk about a red-carpet entrance!

Ptolemy XIII did not live long after a fight with Caesar's army. Cleopatra's brother drowned in the Nile River while running away. She didn't have to worry about a bothersome brother anymore.

Ptolemy XIII

The Nile River

Cleopatra is one of Egypt's most famous pharaohs, but her family wasn't actually Egyptian! Still, she often dressed and spoke like an Egyptian to help earn the peoples' respect.

GUILTY!

It was best to keep your nose out of trouble in ancient Egypt . . . or you might lose it! Some stories tell of criminals having their noses cut off. That's a punishment not to be sniffed at!

Ancient Egyptian law said that people were guilty unless they could prove their innocence.

An ancient funeral

Believe it or not, there were worse punishments than losing your nose. For really serious crimes, you could be refused a proper burial after death. Many people feared that this would keep them from the **afterlife**.

Police in ancient Egypt had a bit of extra help when it came to catching criminals. They trained baboons to help them chase thieves who ran from the law!

You've really made a monkey out of me!

Once the baboon had stopped a criminal, the police would catch up and make the arrest.

Ancient Egyptian police

ADORED ANIMALS

Animals were important in ancient Egypt. Some were even seen as **sacred**. Many Egyptian gods were part human and part animal.

Bastet:
Part cat

Anubis:
Part jackal

Taweret:
Part hippopotamus

Thoth:
Part ibis bird
or baboon

Wadjet:
Part cobra

Sobek:
Part crocodile

MILLIONS OF MUMMIES

In ancient Egypt, all sorts of animals were **mummified** after death. Their bodies were dried out and wrapped in cloth. They were then buried or used as **offerings** to the gods.

A mummified crocodile

CATS

Cats were especially likely to be mummified. People believed the felines had a connection to the goddess Bastet and that they would bring good luck. Cats were so important that the punishment for killing one, even by accident, was death.

When a pet cat passed away, everyone in the household shaved off their eyebrows to **mourn** the loss!

Rich families included jewelry with their mummified pets.

NOTHING'S FAIR IN LOVE AND WAR

The ancient Egyptians' love of animals backfired on them more than once.

CAT CLASH

When the Egyptians were at war with the Persians, the Persian king used a terrible trick to win a battle. He got his army to carry cats with them. Since the Egyptian army did not want to accidentally injure sacred cats, they were quickly defeated.

Meow!

THE SNORE WAR

Cats weren't the only sacred animals that played a part in war. One war was started because some hippopotamuses snored too loudly!

Z
z
z

Apophis of Hyksos threatened to harm the sacred Egyptian hippos that kept him awake with loud snoring. Pharaoh Seqenenre Tao II was not happy about this threat and marched his army to war.

The sacred hippos' pool

The pharaoh was killed in battle, but what happened to the hippos? No one really knows.

We need our shut-eye!

DEATH (AND THE BIT AFTER THAT)

PROFESSIONAL MOURNERS

When some people died in ancient Egypt, their loved ones paid professional mourners to come to the funeral. This showed that the dead person was important.

What did it take to be a professional mourner?
- All mourners were women with no children.
- They had the names of the goddesses Isis and Nephthys tattooed on their shoulders.
- Mourners would cry and pull their hair out to show sadness.

Mourners

Dying may not have been ideal, but many people looked forward to the afterlife. Ancient Egyptians believed they would go to a **paradise** after death.

The ancient Egyptian idea of paradise

Ancient Egyptians believed to get to paradise, you first had to make a dangerous journey through the **underworld**.

They also believed you would be tested by the gods.

One test involved weighing a person's heart. If it weighed the same as a feather, the person would be let into paradise.

Heart

Feather

19

HOW TO MAKE A MUMMY

One of the most important parts of preparing for the afterlife was properly **preserving** the body. What are the steps to make a mummy?

STEP 1: Clean the body.

STEP 2: Take out all the **organs** except the heart.

The brain was removed from the head by picking it out with a hook that was shoved up the nose.

canopic jars

STEP 3: Store the freshly removed organs inside canopic jars.

The Egyptians believed that these organs would be protected in the afterlife.

STEP 4: Cover the body with salt. Let it dry for about 40 days.

STEP 5: Fill the saggy parts of the body with cloth. Add makeup, fake eyes, a wig, and **amulets**.

A fake toe

Missing body parts, such as toes or noses, were sometimes replaced.

STEP 6: Wrap the body in bandages and a sticky material called resin.

STEP 7: Add a mask and place in a coffin.

GRAVE GOODS

People were buried with all the things needed for their journey to the afterlife. These were called grave goods.

SNACKS AND OTHER STUFF

Grave goods being carried to the tomb

People were often buried with food, drinks, clothing, jewelry, games, and even toothbrushes.

SHIPS

Pharaohs believed they needed a boat for their underworld journey. They were often buried with model boats.

Pharaoh Khufu was buried with a full-sized ship!

Ancient Egyptians believed a drawing, model, or even a written description of something would work as a grave good if they couldn't get the real thing.

SHABTI

The ancient Egyptians believed people still had to work in the afterlife. One way around this was to bury shabti dolls with the dead person. These small statues had magic spells painted on them. People believed the spells would bring the dolls to life so they could do all the work instead.

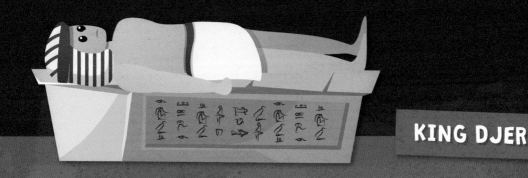

KING DJER

One king took things a step further. Rather than being buried with dolls, he was surrounded by actual human servants!

23

IMPRESSIVE PYRAMIDS

Most ancient Egyptians were buried in graves in the desert, but pharaohs made a bit of extra effort. Many pharaohs had huge stone pyramids built as tombs to be buried in after they died.

King Khufu's pyramid was built out of 2,300,000 massive blocks of stone. It took builders more than 20 years to complete.

Pyramids may have been covered with smooth, white stones. Those blocks have been lost over time.

SUPERNATURAL SPELLS AND MENACING MESSAGES

Ancient Egyptian writing was made up of symbols called hieroglyphs. Some pyramid walls were covered in spells written in hieroglyphs that were meant to help the pharaoh on the journey to the afterlife.

Some pyramids also had written warnings about the punishments that could happen to people who broke into the pharaohs' tombs. Unfortunately, these curses didn't seem to stop many grave robbers.

25

GLAMOROUS GETUP

Ancient Egyptians liked to look good. However, many of their beauty **products** were a little bit . . . strange.

I asked for cornrows, not a corn wig!

WIGS

Wigs were worn both to make people look good and to protect them from the sun. Some were made from real human hair, but most were made out of vegetables.

WAX CONES

Sometimes, people wore a cone of wax on their wigs. No one is completely sure why. Some people think these cones made people smell nice as the wax melted.

SKIN SMOOTHERS

People rubbed oils into their skin to keep it healthy and to stop wrinkles. These oils were so important that they were sometimes given to workers as wages.

MAKEUP

Makeup was also a must. People put black and green powders around their eyes. They believed this would protect them from illnesses.

Red lipstick was made from crushed insects. Making just a small jar of lipstick took tens of thousands of bugs!

27

WEIRD WAYS TO STAY WELL

Ancient Egyptians had many different ways of staying healthy. Some were stranger than others. . . .

AMULETS

Many ancient Egyptians used magic to keep themselves healthy. They wore amulets that were supposed to protect against diseases.

TOOTHPASTE

Toothpaste was invented in ancient Egypt, although the recipe was a little different from that of today's toothpastes. It used ox hoof powder, salt, crushed rocks, and burnt eggshells.

SHEPHERD OF THE ROYAL BOTTOM

One strange job in ancient Egypt was the shepherd of the royal bottom. This person was paid to help when the pharaoh was having trouble on the toilet!

An ancient Egyptian toilet

The shepherd used a long, golden tube to spray water into the pharaoh's behind. Even when the pharaoh was healthy, the shepherd would do this about once a month to help keep everything clean.

SERIOUSLY STRANGE

Ancient Egypt is seriously cool to learn about, but it was also seriously strange. From pharaohs and pyramids to mummies and magic, the people who lived in this peculiar past sure had some terrible tales, surprising stories, and hard-to-believe history!